D1518614

The Beaver

This book has been reviewed
for accuracy by

Walter Plaut, Ph.D.
Professor of Zoology
University of Wisconsin — Madison
and
Frank A. Iwen
Curator, Zoological Museum
University of Wisconsin — Madison

Library of Congress Number: 79-13305

1 2 3 4 5 6 7 8 9 0 83 82 81 80 79

Printed in the United States of America.

Library of Congress Cataloging in Publication Data

Hogan, Paula Z
    The beaver.

    Cover title: The life cycle of the beaver.
    SUMMARY: Describes in simple terms the life cycle
of the beaver.
    1. Beavers — Juvenile literature. [1. Beavers]
I. Miyake, Yoshi. II. Title. III. Title: The life
cycle of the beaver.
QL737.R632H63   599'.3232   79-13305
ISBN 0-8172-1502-6 lib. bdg.

The
BEAVER

By Paula Z. Hogan
Illustrations by Yoshi Miyake

RAINTREE CHILDRENS BOOKS
Milwaukee • Toronto • Melbourne • London

 # The Beaver

Beavers live deep in the forest.
Much of their time is spent in
ponds, for they swim well.

While underwater, beavers close their mouths and ears, keeping water out. Strong, webbed back paws push them forward.

Beavers also use their back paws
to comb their thick, oily fur. Clean
fur helps them stay warm and dry.

During the spring each mother has three or four babies, called kits. Soon after birth the kits swim and play.

The babies follow their mother
as she finds food. Beavers eat
green plants and twigs.

    Once the sun sets, beavers go
to work. Each family builds
and cares for a dam of sticks,
grass, and stones. Mud holds
everything together.

Water backs up behind the dam
and forms a pond. Then beavers
can reach more trees without going
far from the pond's edge.

At times a hungry bear or wolf will come to the pond. The beaver slaps its tail down. That sound warns other beavers to hide underwater.

Beavers leave their first home
at the age of two. They move
downstream, find mates, and build
new homes.

Each fall, beavers ready their
houses for winter. They add more
mud and sticks to keep out
the cold.

pond
surface

vent

living
chamber

tunnel
entrance

Some houses are built in the
middle of the pond. Others are at
the water's edge. A tunnel starts
in the floor of the house and opens
just under the water. Beavers use
the tunnel to go outside.

Beavers cut trees with sharp front teeth. They store the trees underwater and eat them in winter.

Through the long winter
months, beavers stay under the
ice. Only after the ice melts will
they start a new family.

Animals like beavers are called rodents. Their front teeth are very sharp and never stop growing. Muskrats, mice, and squirrels are rodents that live near beaver ponds.

squirrel

muskrat

mouse

31

GLOSSARY

These words are explained the way they are used in this book. Words of more than one syllable are in parentheses. The heavy type shows which syllable is stressed.

dam — a wall that holds back water

downstream (down·stream) — following the flow of the water in a stream

entrance (**en**·trance) — place where something can enter

forest (**for**·est) — trees and plants that cover a large area of land

fur — thick, hairy coat of an animal

kit — a baby beaver

living chamber (**liv**·ing **cham**·ber) — space inside beaver house where beavers live

mate — the male or female of a pair

pond — body of water smaller than a lake

rodent (**ro**·dent) — animal with sharp front teeth, like a beaver, mouse, muskrat, or squirrel

surface (**sur**·face) — the top of a thing

tunnel (**tun**·nel) — long passage under the water

vent — the space where air can enter

webbed — having skin between the toes